Cool Hotels
Spa & Wellness

teNeues

Imprint

Produced by fusion publishing GmbH, Stuttgart . Los Angeles   www.fusion-publishing.com

Editorial team: Martin Nicholas Kunz (Editor + Layout)
Ariane Gerber / Gala Germany (Introduction), Patrice Farameh ("What's special" texts)
Nathalie Grolimund, Anne-Kathrin Meier (Editorial coordination)
Sabine Scholz (Text coordination), Alphagriese (Translation coordination)
Dr. Elisabetta Sangirardi (Italian), Christine Grimm (US-English), Stéphanie Laloix (French), Juan Francisco Lopez (Spanish)
Jan Hausberg, Anke Scholz (Prepress + imaging)

Cover photo (location): courtesy Aman Resorts (Amanyara)

Back cover photos from top to bottom (location): courtesy Voyages Hotels & Resorts (Bedarra Island), courtesy Gräflicher Park Hotel & Spa, courtesy Vatulele Island Resort, Gavin Jackson (Kempinski Hotel Colony Park Plaza), Martin Nicholas Kunz (Hotel Bora Bora)

Photos (location): courtesy Adam & Eve (Adam & Eve Hotels); courtesy Aleenta Phuket – Phangnga; courtesy Aman Resorts (Amanyara); courtesy Bayerischer Hof (Bayerischer Hof pp. 42, 44+45); courtesy Carlisle Bay; courtesy wine & spa resort LOISIUM Hotel (p. 59); Hauke Dresser (wine & spa resort LOISIUM Hotel, pp. 60+61); courtesy Faena Hotel + Universe (Faena Hotel + Universe, pp 206, 209–213); Michelle Galindo (The Standard Miami, p. 169); courtesy German del Sol (Macduff Everton, Juan Pablo Gonzalez, Daniel Gonzalez, Jaime Borquez, Felipe Camus) (Remota); courtesy Gräflicher Park Hotel & Spa; courtesy Grand Hotel Bellevue (Grand Hotel Bellevue p. 63, 65); courtesy Hotel Saint-Barth Isle de France; Gavin Jackson (Kempinski Hotel Colony Park Plaza, Post Ranch Inn, Saman Villas, The Parker Palm Springs); Klaus Frahm, courtesy Side Hamburg (Side); Nicolas Koenig (The Standard Miami, p. 168; Faena Hotel + Universe, pp. 207+208); courtesy Mayflower Inn & Spa; Paul Ott, courtesy Hotel Schwarzer Adler (Schwarzer Adler); Christine Schaum (wine & spa resort LOISIUM Hotel, p.58); courtesy Vatulele Island Resort; courtesy vigilius mountain resort; courtesy Voyages Hotels & Resorts (Bedarra Island)
All other photos by Roland Bauer and Martin Nicholas Kunz

Price orientation: $ < 200 $, $$ 201–350 $, $$$ 351–550 $, $$$$ > 551 $

Published by teNeues Publishing Group

teNeues Verlag GmbH + Co. KG
Am Selder 37
47906 Kempen, Germany
Tel.: 0049-(0)2152-916-0
Fax: 0049-(0)2152-916-111
E-mail: books@teneues.de

teNeues Publishing Company
16 West 22nd Street
New York, NY 10010, USA
Tel.: 001-212-627-9090
Fax: 001-212-627-9511

teNeues Publishing UK Ltd.
P.O. Box 402
West Byfleet
KT14 7ZF, Great Britain
Tel.: 0044-1932-403509
Fax: 0044-1932-403514

teNeues France S.A.R.L.
93, rue Bannier
45000 Orléans, France
Tel.: 0033-2-38541071
Fax: 0033-2-38625340

Press department: arehn@teneues.de
Tel.: 0049-(0)2152-916-202

www.teneues.com

ISBN: 978-3-8327-9243-5

© 2008 teNeues Verlag GmbH + Co. KG, Kempen

Printed in Italy

Bibliographic information published by Die Deutsche Bibliothek.
Die Deutsche Bibliothek lists this publication in the Deutsche Nationalbibliografie;
detailed bibliographic data is available in the Internet at http://dnb.ddb.de.

Contents   Page

Introduction   5

The Grove	10	Four Seasons Bali at Sayan	110
Stoke Park Club	16	Bedarra Island	114
Gräflicher Park Hotel & Spa	20	Vatulele Island Resort	120
Villa Kennedy	26	Hotel Bora Bora	126
Side	32	Sheraton Moorea Lagoon	138
Kempinski Grand Hotel		The Parker Palm Springs	146
Heiligendamm	36	Post Ranch Inn	152
Bayerischer Hof	42	Sanctuary on Camelback	
Grand Spa Resort A-ROSA		Mountain	158
Kitzbühel	46	Mayflower Inn & Spa	164
Schwarzer Adler	50	The Standard Miami	168
wine & spa resort LOISIUM Hotel	58	The Tides Riviera Maya	174
Grand Hotel Bellevue	62	Amanyara	180
Victoria Jungfrau	66	Carlisle Bay	188
Therme Vals	72	Hotel Saint-Barth Isle de France	196
vigilius mountain resort	76	Kempinski Hotel Colony	
Adam & Eve Hotels	80	Park Plaza	200
Amanjena	86	Faena Hotel + Universe	206
The Oberoi Udaivilas	92	Remota	214
Saman Villas	98		
Aleenta Phuket – Phangnga	104	Map	220

Introduction

Travel is good for you. It frees your mind, elevates your soul, and simply takes you farther. Sometimes even just a weekend in different surroundings is enough to allow you return to everyday life with recharged batteries and a refreshed feeling. It's fun to discover unusual hotspots and conquer unknown areas. If you are looking for more than just temporary inspiration, you can also find it. In the ideal case, you will go on a journey to yourself. The best way to do this is to free yourself from apparent constraints and keep your eye on your true needs so that you also pay attention to your soul. The best spas in the world have sensitive therapists who make sure that you find your way back to yourself. If you have the feeling of being in the right place at the right time, this is the perfect precondition for recuperation. Traditional therapies and beauty rituals make the attitude toward life and the essence of the respective country tangible. For example, the Balinese massage becomes that country's typical pleasure in a pure culture at the *Four Seasons Bali at Sayan*.

But you no longer need to travel half way around the world when searching for a holistic cultural exchange. Fusion not only sets the tone in the area of gastronomy, but also when in terms of wellness. One example is the *Blue Spa* at the *Bayerischer Hof* in Munich, which offers exotic massages by international specialists. In the meantime, the best from the Orient and the Occident can be found in the treatments offered by *Adam & Eve* in Belek on the Turkish Riviera. For people who are especially stressed, it even has ten so-called spa suites: with their own sauna, treatment room, Turkish bath, and bedroom. But some people also use the health concepts recommended by the well-being experts to develop a lifestyle that extends into their everyday lives. Guests of the *Mayflower Inn & Spa* in Washington, Connecticut are provided with creativity training and an extensive coaching program for coping with stress. The 30-room retreat in the English country-house style offers the perfect framework for re-establishing the balance of work and life. This book serves as an orientation for where the journey can go: 37 cool top spots for one-day visits or entire wellness vacations.

Ariane Gerber (Gala Germany)

Einleitung

Reisen tut gut. Es macht den Kopf frei, beflügelt die Seele und bringt uns einfach weiter. Manchmal reicht schon ein Wochenende in einer anderen Umgebung, um neu aufzutanken und erfrischt in den Alltag zurückzukehren. Es macht Spaß, ungewöhnliche Hotspots zu entdecken und fremde Gegenden zu erobern. Auch wer mehr sucht als zeitweilige Inspiration wird fündig. Im Idealfall gelangen wir durch Reisen zu uns selbst. Dabei müssen wir eigentlich nur darauf achten, dass wir uns von vermeintlichen Zwängen frei machen und unsere wirklichen Bedürfnisse nicht aus dem Blick verlieren, damit unsere Seele nicht auf der Strecke bleibt. In den besten Spas der Welt sorgen einfühlsame Therapeuten dafür, dass wir wieder zu uns selbst finden. Wenn sich das Gefühl einstellt, zur richtigen Zeit am richtigen Ort zu sein, ist das die perfekte Voraussetzung zum Erholen. Traditionelle Therapien und Schönheitsrituale machen das Lebensgefühl und das Wesen des jeweiligen Landes spürbar. Die balinesische Massage z. B. wird im *Four Seasons Bali at Sayan* zum landestypischen Genuss in Reinkultur.

Inzwischen braucht man auf der Suche nach ganzheitlichem Kulturaustausch aber längst nicht mehr um den halben Globus zu reisen. Denn Fusion gibt nicht nur im Gastrobereich, sondern auch in Sachen Wellness den Ton an. So wartet etwa der *Blue Spa* im *Bayerischen Hof* in München beim Angebot exotischer Massagen mit internationalen Spezialisten auf. Das Beste aus Orient und Okzident findet sich derweil im Treatment-Angebot des *Adam & Eve* in Belek an der türkischen Riviera. Für besonders Gestresste gibt es dort sogar zehn sogenannte Spa-Suiten: mit eigener Sauna, Behandlungsraum, türkischem Bad und Schlafzimmer. Manch einer nutzt die angebotenen Gesundheitskonzepte der Wohlfühlexperten aber auch, um sich eine Lebensweise anzueignen, die bis in den Alltag hineinreicht. Kreativitäts-Training und ein umfangreiches Coaching-Programm zur Stressbewältigung werden z. B. den Gästen des *Mayflower Inn & Spa* in Washington, Connecticut, vermittelt. Das 30-Zimmer-Retreat im englischen Landhausstil bietet den perfekten Rahmen, um die Work-Life-Balance wieder herzustellen. Dieses Buch dient zur Orientierung, wohin die Reise gehen kann: 37 coole Top-Adressen für Tagesbesuche oder ganze Wellnessurlaube.

Ariane Gerber (Gala Germany)

Introduction

Voyager vous fait du bien. Cela vous dégage l'esprit, vous libère l'âme et vous fait mûrir. Parfois, il suffit d'un weekend dans un cadre différent pour se ressourcer et revenir plein d'énergie à sa vie quotidienne. C'est passionnant de découvrir des coins insolites et de s'approprier des lieux inconnus. Et si vous cherchez plus qu'une source d'inspiration passagère, c'est aussi ce que vous trouverez. Dans le meilleur des cas, le voyage vous permettra de vous trouver vous-même ; pour cela, il faudra vous libérer des contraintes apparentes et rester concentré sur vos réels besoins, pour finalement atteindre votre âme. Les meilleurs *spas* du monde disposent de thérapeutes compétents qui se chargeront de vous faire retrouver le chemin vers vous-même. Pour bien se reposer, il faut sentir que vous êtes au bon endroit, au bon moment. Les thérapies traditionnelles et les rituels de beauté rendent tangibles l'art de vivre et l'essence de chaque pays. Le massage du *Four Seasons Bali at Sayan*, par exemple, traduit un plaisir propre à la culture balinaise la plus authentique.

Mais vous n'avez plus besoin de parcourir la moitié du monde pour trouver un dépaysement culturel complet. La fusion n'est pas seulement un concept à la mode en gastronomie, elle se répand aussi dans le monde du bien-être. Le *Blue Spa* du *Bayerischer Hof* de Munich propose dans son offre des massages exotiques effectués par des spécialistes internationaux. Parallèlement, le meilleur de l'Orient et de l'Occident se rencontrent dans les soins proposés par l'*Adam & Eve* à Belek, sur la Riviera turque. Ceux qui souffrent particulièrement du stress peuvent profiter d'une des dix « suites spa », disposant d'un sauna, d'une salle de soin, d'un hammam et d'une chambre. Mais certains appliquent les concepts de santé recommandés par les experts du bien-être en les intégrant dans leur style de vie quotidien. Le *Mayflower Inn & Spa* de Washington, dans le Connecticut, propose à ses clients une formation créative conjuguée à un programme d'entrainement complet pour combattre le stress. Ce refuge au style rustique anglais, avec ses 30 chambres, constitue le cadre parfait pour retrouver l'équilibre entre vie professionnelle et personnelle. Cet ouvrage vous servira de guide pour prévoir votre voyage, avec 37 destinations *cools* idéales pour une journée ou des vacances complètes sous le signe du bien-être.

Ariane Gerber (Gala Germany)

Introducción

Viajar sienta bien. Despeja la cabeza, libera el alma y nos hace madurar. En ocasiones, basta con salir un fin de semana a otro tipo de ambiente para cargar baterías y volver con energías renovadas al quehacer diario. Resulta emocionante descubrir rincones insólitos y hacerse con lugares desconocidos. También aquel que busque algo más que una inspiración pasajera, se verá recompensado. En el mejor de los casos, un viaje sirve para llegar al fondo de uno mismo. Es entonces cuando habría que procurar liberarse de las supuestas ataduras y no desatender las auténticas necesidades, con el fin de que nuestra alma complete la travesía iniciada. Los mejores *spas* del mundo cuentan con complacientes terapeutas que se encargan de que nos volvamos a reencontrar con nosotros mismos. Mentalizarse de que uno se encuentra en el lugar y el momento adecuados es el requisito perfecto para un buen descanso. Las terapias tradicionales y los rituales de belleza son una extensión de los sentimientos y del carácter de cada país. El masaje balinés del *Four Seasons Bali at Sayan* es, por ejemplo, todo un placer propio de la cultura autóctona más tradicional.

Desde hace algún tiempo, aquellos que buscan un completo intercambio cultural no necesitan recorrerse medio mundo para conseguirlo. La fusión no solo está de moda en el ámbito de la restauración, sino también en el mundo del *wellness*. Siguiendo esta línea, el *Blue Spa* del *Bayerischer Hof* de Múnich cuenta en su oferta con masajes exóticos a cargo de especialistas internacionales. Por su parte, lo mejor de Oriente y Occidente se puede encontrar en la oferta de cuidados del *Adam & Eve* de Belek, en la Riviera turca. Para aquellos que padezcan especialmente de estrés, dispondrán aquí de diez de las llamadas "spa-suites", con su propia sauna, su sala de tratamiento, baño turco y dormitorio. Más de uno aprovechará los paquetes de salud ofertados por los expertos en sensación de bienestar con el fin de conseguir un estado emocional que permita sobrellevar la vuelta a la rutina diaria. Un entrenamiento que fomenta la creatividad junto a un extenso programa personalizado para combatir el estrés son algunas de las posibilidades que se brindan a los huéspedes del *Mayflower Inn & Spa* de Washington (Connecticut). Este retiro de estilo rústico, con sus 30 alcobas, constituye el marco perfecto para conseguir alcanzar de nuevo el equilibrio entre vida laboral y personal. El presente volumen le servirá de guía para decidir el curso de su viaje: 37 destinos de primer orden donde pasar una jornada o disfrutar de unas completas vacaciones *wellness*.

Ariane Gerber (Gala Germany)

Introduzione

Viaggiare fa bene. Libera la testa, mette le ali all'anima e ci porta semplicemente avanti. A volte basta già un fine settimana in un ambiente diverso per ricaricarsi e ritornare rivitalizzati nella vita di tutti i giorni. E' divertente scoprire le straordinarie località popolari e conquistare terre straniere. Anche chi cerca di più di una momentanea ispirazione, trova. Nel caso ideale attraverso i viaggi ritroviamo noi stessi. Dobbiamo soltanto stare attenti a liberarci di eventuali costrizioni e non perdere di vista le nostre necessità, per non perdere la nostra anima lungo la via. Nelle migliori spa del mondo sono i terapeuti sensibili a curarsi di noi, per farci ritrovare noi stessi. Se abbiamo la sensazione di essere al posto giusto al momento giusto, questo è la premessa perfetta per rilassarsi. Le terapie tradizionali e i rituali di bellezza rendono palpabile la gioia di vivere e l'essenza del relativo paese. Il massaggio balinese per esempio diventa nel *Four Seasons Bali at Sayan* un tipico piacere autentico del luogo.

Intanto non si deve più viaggiare per mezzo mondo per cercare uno scambio completo di cultura. Infatti, la fusione pone l'accento non soltanto nell'ambito gastronomico ma anche in fatto di benessere. Così per esempio il *Blue Spa* nel *Bayerischer Hof* a Monaco presenta un'offerta di massaggi esotici fatti da specialisti internazionali. Attualmente si può trovare il meglio dell'oriente e dell'occidente nell'offerta di trattamenti del *Adam & Eve* di Belek sulla riviera turca. Per le persone particolarmente stressate esistono dieci cosiddette Spa-Suite: con sauna propria, studio medico, bagno turco e camera da letto. Qualcuno si serve dei concetti di salute offerti dagli esperti del benessere, per appropriarsi anche di un modo di vivere che si propaga fino alla vita di tutti i giorni. Nel *Mayflower Inn & Spa* di Washington (Connecticut) viene proposto agli ospiti, per esempio un training creativo e un ampio programma di allenamento per la mente per smantellare lo stress. Il ritiro con 30 camere in stile campagnolo inglese offre la cornice perfetta per ristabilire l'equilibrio tra lavoro e vita. Questo libro serve come guida sul dove ci può portare un viaggio: 37 indirizzi di posti meravigliosi, primi in classifica, per visite giornaliere oppure intere vacanze di benessere.

Ariane Gerber (Gala Germany)

The Grove

Chandler's Cross
WD3 4TG Hertfordshire
United Kingdom
Phone: +441923807807
Fax: +441923221008
www.thegrove.co.uk

Price category: $$$$
Rooms: 227 rooms and suites
Facilities: 3 restaurants and bars, garden terraces, pools, meetings & event facilities, golf course, Ayurvedic spa, gym, jacuzzi, sauna, heat treatments, kid's club
Services: Babysitting, laundry services, 24h room service, turn down service, WiFi access, business center
Located: Easy national and international access from Heathrow (30 minutes), Gatwick (60 minutes), Luton (30 minutes) and Stansted (60 minutes) airports
Map: No. 1
Style: Modern country chic
What's special: Traditional country house elegance combined with 21st century design; has views over a beautiful 120 hectares estate and its championship golf course; the award-winning spa Sequoia has state-of-the-art fitness facilities, including a black-tiled mosaic pool.

Stoke Park Club

Park Road, Stoke Poges
SL2 4PG Buckinghamshire
United Kingdom
Phone: +441753717171
Fax: +441753717181
www.stokeparkclub.com

Price category: $$$
Rooms: 21 rooms and suites (28 new rooms to open in May 2008)
Facilities: 4 restaurants, 2 bars, SPA SPC, golf course, tennis courts, gymnasium
Services: Satellite television, direct dial telephones, broadband
Located: Nearest Airport: London Heathrow (11 km)
Map: No. 2
Style: Classic elegance
What's special: Set within 350 acres of parkland and historic gardens, the suites have been designed with priceless antiques and original paintings, including marble bathrooms with heated floors and cast iron baths; the club combines sumptuous luxury with the country's finest sporting and leisure facilities.

Gräflicher Park Hotel & Spa

Brunnenallee 1
33014 Bad Driburg
Germany
Phone: +49525395230
Fax: +4952539523205
www.graeflicher-park.de

Price category: $$
Rooms: 135 rooms and suites
Facilities: 2 restaurants, fusion bar, spa area featuring steam baths, saunas, several treatments, gym, heated 25 meters long outdoor pool, big whirlpool
Services: Babysitter service, wireless internet, arrangement of transportation, 18-holes golf course
Located: 35 km from airport Paderborn, 150 km from Hannover airport, ICE train station Altenbeken
Map: No. 3
Style: Modern country chic
What's special: This 226 years old spa resort combines traditional country house elegance with modern design. All the rooms and spa facilities overlook the 65 hectares landscape park. The award-winning spa offers treatments based on the own mineral spring. Exclusive private spa suites, spacious relaxation areas give the feeling of luxury.

Villa Kennedy

Rocco Forte Collection
Kennedyallee 70
60596 Frankfurt
Germany
Phone: +4969717120
Fax: +4969717122430
www.villakennedy.com

Price category: $$$$
Rooms: 163 rooms including 28 suites and 1 presidential suite
Services: Free WiFi in public area, 24h room-service, 9 conference rooms, ballroom
Located: 20 minutes from Frankfurt International Airport
Map: No. 4
Style: Contemporary design
What's special: Spacious suites have lounge and dining areas, walk-in closets and separate guest washrooms, and the latest technology such as flat-screen televisions. The Villa Spa has an indoor pool and treatment rooms with relaxing views overlooking a lush garden.

Side

Drehbahn 49
20354 Hamburg
Germany
Phone: +4940309990
Fax: +494030999399
www.side-hamburg.de

Price category: $$
Rooms: 178 rooms and suites
Facilities: Fusion bar + restaurant, sky lounge includir
terrace located on the 8th floor and overlooking Hamb
spa area featuring pool with jacuzzi, steam bath, saur
solarium, wellbeing with cardio equipment and power
plates, massages and cosmetic treatments
Services: Wireless internet, babysitting service, hand
capped rooms/facilities, pets allowed
Located: 10 km from airport
Map: No. 5
Style: Contemporary design
What's special: The minimalist design includes a 12
story tower of glass and natural stone with a colorful
display of light installations. The spa offers massage
in color therapy rooms for various ailments, and an
aromatic steam bath for increased circulation.

Kempinski Grand Hotel Heiligendamm

Prof.-Dr.-Vogel-Straße 16-18
18209 Bad Doberan – Heiligen-
damm
Germany
Phone: +49382037400
Fax: +49382037407474
www.kempinski-heiligendamm.com

Price category: $$$
Rooms: 215 rooms and suites
Facilities: 4 restaurants, 3 bars, sauna world, spa, pool,
ballroom
Services: Airport shuttle, babysitting services, bridal
suite, packed lunches, free wireless
Located: directly at the beach of the Baltic Sea in
Mecklenburg-Western Pomerania, near Rostock
Map: No. 6
Style: Modern classic
What's special: This majestic building has a 3,000 m²
wellness area in its own palatial space, including a medi-
cal spa; a separate children's area includes the "Polar
Bear Club" with private villas and activities such as pony
riding, pirate parties, and story telling.

Promenadeplatz 2-6
80333 Munich
Germany
Phone: +498921200
Fax: +49892120906
www.bayerischerhof.de

Price category: $$$$
Rooms: 373 rooms including 60 suites
Facilities: 4 restaurants, 6 bars, 40 conference rooms, "Blue Spa", beauty center, hair salon with hair spa, theater "Kömodie im Bayerischen Hof", night club
Services: High speed internet access, disabled facilities, business center, 24h concierge-service, 24h parking
Located: in the center of Munich next to Marienplatz, 35-minutes drive to the airport
Map: No. 7
Style: Classic elegance
What's special: The city's wellness oasis is in the midst of a lush rooftop garden with a turquoise-blue pool with breathtaking views over the picturesque old town. The "Blue Spa" offers a wide range of services, such as fitness on state-of-the-art equipment to special body treatments.

Grand Spa Resort A-ROSA Kitzbühel

Ried Kaps 7
6370 Kitzbühel
Austria
Phone: +43535665660980
Fax: +43535665660819
www.a-rosa.de

Price category: $$$$
Rooms: 104 rooms and 46 suites
Facilities: Restaurant "STREIF", Restaurant "KAPS", golfhouse restaurant, "Marktplatz" bar and lounge area, 4 conference rooms for up to 200 people, business center, dedicated golf concierge, sports and golf shop with ski and golf hire, hairdresser, shop
Services: Mineral water in the room, internet access
Located: in excellent position above the town center of Kitzbühel in the direct vicinity of the Kitzbühel golf course
Map: No. 8
Style: Classic elegance
What's special: Reminiscent of a Tyrolean castle, this resort is set right on the Kitzbühel Golf Course and has stunning views over the Alps. Its very unique spa is made especially for A-ROSA and offers a complete health concept.

Schwarzer Adler

Florianigasse 15
6370 Kitzbühel
Austria
Phone: +4353566911
Fax: +43535673939
www.adlerkitz.at

Price category: $$$$
Rooms: 88 rooms and suites
Facilities: Lobby with open fire place and bar, fine dining restaurant with 1 star Michelin, main restaurant, "Black Spa" with saunas, steambath, relaxation areas and beauty center, large panorama fitness center
Services: Secretarial service, free wireless in lobby
Located: 1-hour drive from Salzburg and Innsbruck airports and 2-hours drive from Munich airport
Map: No. 9
Style: Classic elegance
What's special: The hotel dates back to the 17th century and offers an atmosphere of Tyrolean hospitality and charm, with luxurious rooms with private sauna. The 1.500 m² spa includes the largest rooftop pool of the Alps and an indoor pool with light and underwater sound system.

wine & spa resort LOISIUM Hotel

Loisium Allee 2
3550 Langenlois
Austria
Phonel: +43273477100200
Fax: + 43273477100100
www.loisiumhotel.at

Price category: $
Rooms: 82 rooms
Facilities: Restaurant "Vineyard", "Holl Bar", "Aveda Wine Spa"
Located: in the vineyards, close to the town center of Langenlois
Map: No. 10
Style: Modern
What's special: The high-concept modern hotel with its visitor center which is built on centuries-old wine cellars with stone passages that are over 900 years old, offer stunning views over Austrian wine country. The "Aveda Wine Spa" makes creative use of light to give the space a relaxing, airy feel.

Grand Hotel Bellevue

Hauptstrasse
3780 Gstaad
Switzerland
Phone: +41337480000
Fax: +41337480001
www.bellevue-gstaad.ch

Price category: $$$$
Rooms: 52 rooms and 5 suites
Facilities: 2 restaurants, bars, private cinema, clubhouse, 2500 m² Bellevue Spa
Services: Disabled access, garage, free internet access
Located: 90-minutes drive to Geneva airport, 2-hours drive to Zurich airport
Map: No. 11
Style: Classic elegance
What's special: Set in the middle of a park, the hotel boasts a private cinema, a nightclub, and a wine cellar with more than 10,000 bottles. The Japanese-style spa provides the ultimate escape to enjoy the restorative effects of Asian body treatments.

Victoria Jungfrau

Höheweg 41
3800 Interlaken
Switzerland
Phone: +41338282828
Fax: +41338282880
www.victoria-jungfrau.ch

Price category: $$$$
Rooms: 212 rooms and suites
Facilities: Restaurant "La Terrasse" (French cuisine), "The Jungfrau Brasserie" (traditional and new Swiss dishes), "La Pastateca" (international pasta and noodle dishes), spa bar
Services: Babysitting service, free internet
Located: 45 minutes from Bern airport, 2.5 hours from Zurich airport, 3 hours from Geneva airport
Map: No. 12
Style: Classic elegance
What's special: The exclusive ESPA offers private treatment rooms and a healthy spa bar; each spa experience has been designed to encompass all aspects of healing from holistic treatments to hydrotherapy in an outdoor saltwater jacuzzi overlooking the surrounding mountains.

Therme Vals

7132 Vals
Switzerland
Phone: +41819268080
Fax: +41819268000
www.therme-vals.ch

Price category: $
Rooms: 60 rooms, new designed by Peter Zumthor
Facilities: Therme spa designed by Peter Zumthor
Located: 20-minutes drive to Chur
Map: No. 13
Style: Contemporary design
What's special: Decorated in Zumthor's spare style, this purist haven is built from 60,000 stone slabs of Valser quartzite. The open and enclosed spaces and linear elements make for a highly sensuous and restorative experience when bathing in one of the spa's six thermal springs.

vigilius mountain resort

Mount S. Vigilius
39011 Lana
Italy
Phone: +390473556600
Fax: +390473556699
www.vigilius.it

Price category: $$$
Rooms: 35 rooms and 6 suites
Facilities: 2 restaurants, library, yoga room, boccia court
Services: move & explore (free activity program), Five Tibetan, archery, shiatsu & watsu, wine tasting, yoga
Located: Accessible by cablecar from Lana
Map: No. 14
Style: Modern country chic
What's special: At 1,500 m above the earth and accessible only by cablecar, this isolated resort in the South Tyrolean Mountains offers a healing spa menu that includes an amazing sauna with view, an outdoor whirlpool amidst the larch forest or an endless pool with a marvellous panorama.

Belek
Antalya
Turkey
Call center: +902424440596
Fax: +902427101414
www.adamevehotels.com

Price category: $$$$
Rooms: 444 rooms, 29 suites, 21 villas and 3 residences
Facilities: 8 restaurants, 8 bars, 5.500 m² spa, fitness center, 7 pools, 4.500 m² convention center, indoor and outdoor sport complex, 4 tennis courts, shopping arcade
Services: Butler service, spa suite service, VIP service, babysitting services, disabled access, game room
Located: in a forest area (100.000 m²) of Belek, Antalya, right on the seaside
Map: No. 15
Style: Contemporary design
What's special: The view stretches across one of the worlds largest pools to merge with the sea and disappear into the horizon. The 5.500 m² "EdenSpa" includes hammam with color therapy and a unique concept called "spa suites" complete with your very own spa butler.

Amanjena

Route de Quarzazate, km 12
Marrakesh
Morocco, 4000
BP 2405, Poste principale de
Gueliz
Phone: +21224403353
Fax: +21224403477
www.amanresorts.com

Price category: $$$$
Rooms: 32 pavilions and 6 maisons
Facilities: Restaurants, bar, library, swimming pool,
health & beauty center, boutiques, tennis courts
Services: Babysitting, translation service, free internet
access
Located: 15-minutes drive to airport
Map: No. 16
Style: Contemporary Moroccan
What's special: Sunset-colored private pavilions are
spacious, some with their own private pools, all with
multi-faceted high domes and wood-burning sunken fires.
Enjoy a traditional hammam, a dip in a glass whirlpool, or
a Moroccan-style body scrub in a private treatment room.

The Oberoi Udaivilas

Haridasji Ki Magri
Udaipur, 313001
Rajasthan
India
Phone: +912942433300
Fax: +912942433200
www.oberoihotels.com

Price category: $$$$
Rooms: 87 rooms and suites
Facilities: In-room check-in, The Oberoi Spa & Fitness Centre, complimentary airport/railway station transfers
Services: Babysitting service, 24h private butler service, business services
Located: The Oberoi Udaivilas is located on the banks of Lake Pichola, 45-minutes drive from Udaipur Airport
Map: No. 17
Style: Classic elegance
What's special: In a city of majestic palaces and beautiful lakes, the palatial architecture of the resort also includes heated private pools and a beautiful spa in a miniature-domed palace that offers a range of luxurious Ayurvedic treatments. A wildlife conservatory, adjacent to the resort, houses the Indian spotted deer, wild boar and peacocks.

Saman Villas

Aturuwella
Bentota
Sri Lanka
Phone: +94342275435
Fax: +94342275433
www.samanvilla.com

Price category: $$$
Rooms: 26 suites (some with private pool) and 1 villa, all with balcony or terrace
Facilities: 2 restaurants, 2 bars, infinity edge pool, luxury garden spa, gym, library, pool table, jewellery shop
Services: 24h room service, taxi service, tour arrangements
Located: Approximately traveling time from airport to hotel is 180 minutes by road and 45 minutes by air
Map: No. 18
Style: Inspired by Sri Lankan architecture and temple design
What's special: The resort is perched on a rocky headland that divides two endless beaches so that each suite provides spectacular views of the shoreline and sea. The "Sahana Spa" is set in a water garden and offers special mud bath treatments in its deluxe suites.

Aleenta Phuket – Phangnga

33 Mu Khokkloy
82140 Khao Pilai Beach, Kok Kloy
Phangnga
Thailand
Phone: +6625085333
Fax: +6625085349
www.aleenta.com

Price category: $$$$
Rooms: 15 suites and 15 villas
Facilities: Restaurant, bar, beach lounge, spa, massages, yoga
Services: Free internet access, babysitting service, fitness center, cooking classes
Located: 20-minutes drive from Phuket airport
Map: No. 19
Style: Contemporary design
What's special: This ultra-private resort has just 30 luxurious suites and villas, with a variety of different accommodations including private pools. The spa features private treatment rooms using only exclusive and 100% natural products and essential oils.

Four Seasons Bali at Sayan

Sayan
80571 Bali
Indonesia
Phone: +62361977577
Fax: +62361977588
www.fourseasons.com/sayan/

Price category: $$$$
Rooms: 18 suites and 42 villas
Facilities: 4 treatment rooms, fitness, shop
Services: Translation services, wireless internet access
Located: 1 hour to Ngurah Rai International Airport
Map: No. 20
Style: Modern classic
What's special: The entire resort reflects the exotic surroundings by featuring Indonesian furnishings and a two-level swimming pool surrounded by a tropical haven. The spa has a variety of treatments from both the East and the West, complete with hot and cold plunge pools.

Bedarra Island

Bedarra Island
North Queensland
Australia
Phone: +61282968010
Fax: +61292992103
www.bedarraisland.com

Price category: $$$$
Rooms: 16 villas
Facilities: Open terrace restaurant included in tariff, 24h lounge and bar, therapeutic massage
Services: Gourmet picnic hampers for beachside lunches, fishing gear, internet access
Located: Regular flights are available from all major Australian cities to Cairns. Transfer to Bedarra Island via a scenic flight to Dunk Island (45 minutes) and a launch transfer from Dunk Island to Bedarra Island (20 minutes)
Map: No. 21
Style: Contemporary tropical design
What's special: Covering 100 hectares, each of the 16 open-plan villas, some glass-walled, are tucked in the rainforest. Only minutes from the ocean, each guest can indulge in a therapeutic massage on the private beach.

Vatulele Island
Fiji
Phone: +6796720300
Fax: +6796720062
www.sixsenses.com

Price category: $$$$
Rooms: 17 villas
Facilities: "Gold Palm PADI Dive Center", wine cellar, organic vegetable garden, restaurant plus private dining, excursions, water activities
Services: Spa treatments, internet access, butlers, weddings
Located: 25-minutes flight from Nadi International Airport
Map: No. 22
Style: Tropical chic
What's special: This perfect tropical oasis accommodates just 19 couples who are pampered by 110 staff members. This 'bare-foot' luxury resort has villas with large open terraces that are a few steps away from the beach, and offers scuba diving and spectacular seafood.

Vatulele Island Resort   123

Hotel Bora Bora

Pointe Raititi, B.P.1, Nunue,
Bora Bora
French Polynesia 98730
Phone: +689604460
Fax: +689604466
www.amanresorts.com

Price category: $$$$
Rooms: 54 bungalows and fares
Facilities: Restaurant, bars, boutique, library, jewellery,
tennis court
Services: Massage and beauty treatment in bungalow,
internet access
Located: 45-minutes flight from Papeete to local airport
on Motu Motu, then 20-minutes transfer by speed boat
Map: No. 23
Style: Contemporary Polynesian
What's special: This Polynesian style luxury hotel was
the first on the island of Bora Bora to introduce over-
water bungalows. Local musicians and dancers provide
Polynesian cultural entertainment. Guests can enjoy
many water-based activities, tennis, or have a massage
in the privacy of their own beach villa.

Sheraton Moorea Lagoon

B.P. 1005 Papetoai, Moorea
French Polynesia
Phone: +689551111
Fax: +689551155
www.sheratonmoorea.com

Price category: $$$$
Rooms: 54 overwater bungalows and 52 garden and beach bungalows
Facilities: Restaurant, bar & grill, 2 bars, each bungalow features a private outdoor shower with unparalleled views, water activities, spa & fitness, boutique, events and weddings with menues
Services: Internet access, horseback riding
Located: 10-minutes flight or 30-minutes catamaran ride from Tahiti
Map: No. 24
Style: Tropical
What's special: Its enchanting dramatic landscapes and bright green valleys make this resort the most beautiful liquid playground in the South Pacific. The unique overwater bungalows have special in-floor glass windows to watch the underwater ballet of tropical fish.

The Parker Palm Springs

4200 East Palm Canyon Drive
92264 Palm Springs, CA
USA
Phone: +17607705000
www.theparkerpalmsprings.com

Price category: $$$$
Rooms: 144 (131 rooms, 12 villas and the "Gene Autry House" – 2 bedroom house on property)
Facilities: 3 restaurants ("NORMA'S" serving breakfast all day, "mister parker's" a french bistro and the "lemonade stand" serving cocktails), 4 red clay tennis courts, 4 pools (2 indoor), 1,400 m² spa, "Palm Springs Yacht Club"
Services: Wake-up calls, wireless internet access, newspaper delivery
Located: in Palm Springs (10 minutes from the downtown area), 2-hours drive from Los Angeles and San Diego
Map: No. 25
Style: Modern classic
What's special: This estate in the desert is set amongst 13 gardens in which you can play croquet and petanque in our lounge on the outdoor hammocks.

Post Ranch Inn

Highway 1
93920 Big Sur, CA
USA
Phone: +18316672200
Fax: +18316672512
www.postranchinn.com

Price category: $$$$
Rooms: 40 rooms
Facilities: "Sierra Mar" restaurant, 2 infinity basking pools, heated lap pool, fitness room, spa treatments, complimentary guided hikes, yoga class
Services: Free parking, internet access
Located: 1-hour drive from Monterey airport, 2.5-hours drive from San Francisco
Map: No. 26
Style: Organic chic
What's special: Perched 380 m above the sea on a cliff, all of the tree-house rooms have a cozy fireplace and private deck. Amenities include in-room spa treatments, large slate spa tub with wideangle mountain or ocean views. Complimentary gourmet breakfast buffet.

Sanctuary on Camelback Mountain

5700 East McDonald Drive
85253 Paradise Valley, AZ
USA
Phone: +14809482100
www.sanctuaryaz.com

Price category: $$$$
Rooms: 98 casitas
Facilities: "elements" restaurant and "jade bar", Arizona's largest infinity-edge pool, Asian-inspired spa with indoor-outdoor treatment rooms, fitness center with movement studio, meditation garden and lap pool, tennis courts, salon, private home collection
Services: HiFi and WiFi internet access, 24h room service, in-room spa treatments, guided hikes and bike-rides
Located: 15 minutes to Phoenix's international airport and 5 minutes from downtown Scottsdale
Map: No. 27
Style: Rustic elegance
What's special: This luxury boutique hideaway with marvelous mountain and spa casitas is an intimate retreat, offering Asian-inspired treatments along with a relaxing meditation garden, movement studio and fitness center.

Mayflower Inn & Spa

118 Woodbury Road
06793 Washington, CT
USA
Phone: +18608689466
Fax: +18608681497
www.mayflowerinn.com

Price category: $$$$
Rooms: 30 rooms
Facilities: Award-winning spa, meeting rooms, indoor & outdoor pool, tennis, hiking, biking
Services: Wireless flat screen TV, fitness nutrition and wellness
Located: 2-hours drive from New York City and area airports
Map: No. 28
Style: Classic elegance
What's special: With its dreamy beds and green-hedged gardens, this hotel welcomes guests into an environment of pure escape and serenity; offering a full range of activities and opportunities to align mind, body, and spirit.

The Standard Miami

40 Island Avenue
33139 Miami, FL
USA
Phone: +13056731717
www.standardhotels.com

Price category: $$$$
Rooms: 105 rooms
Facilities: Pool, spa, gym, indoor restaurant & bayside grill, yoga center, mud lounge, garden
Services: In-room treatments, wireless internet access, 24h room service
Located: 30 minutes from Miami airport
Map: No. 29
Style: Contemporary design
What's special: Taking over the old Lido Spa, this mid-century Miami modernist resort inspires to revive the bathhouse culture with waterfall hot tubs, a mud lounge, and outdoor yoga lawns. Each stylish room is designed with a modern décor and Scandinavian furniture.

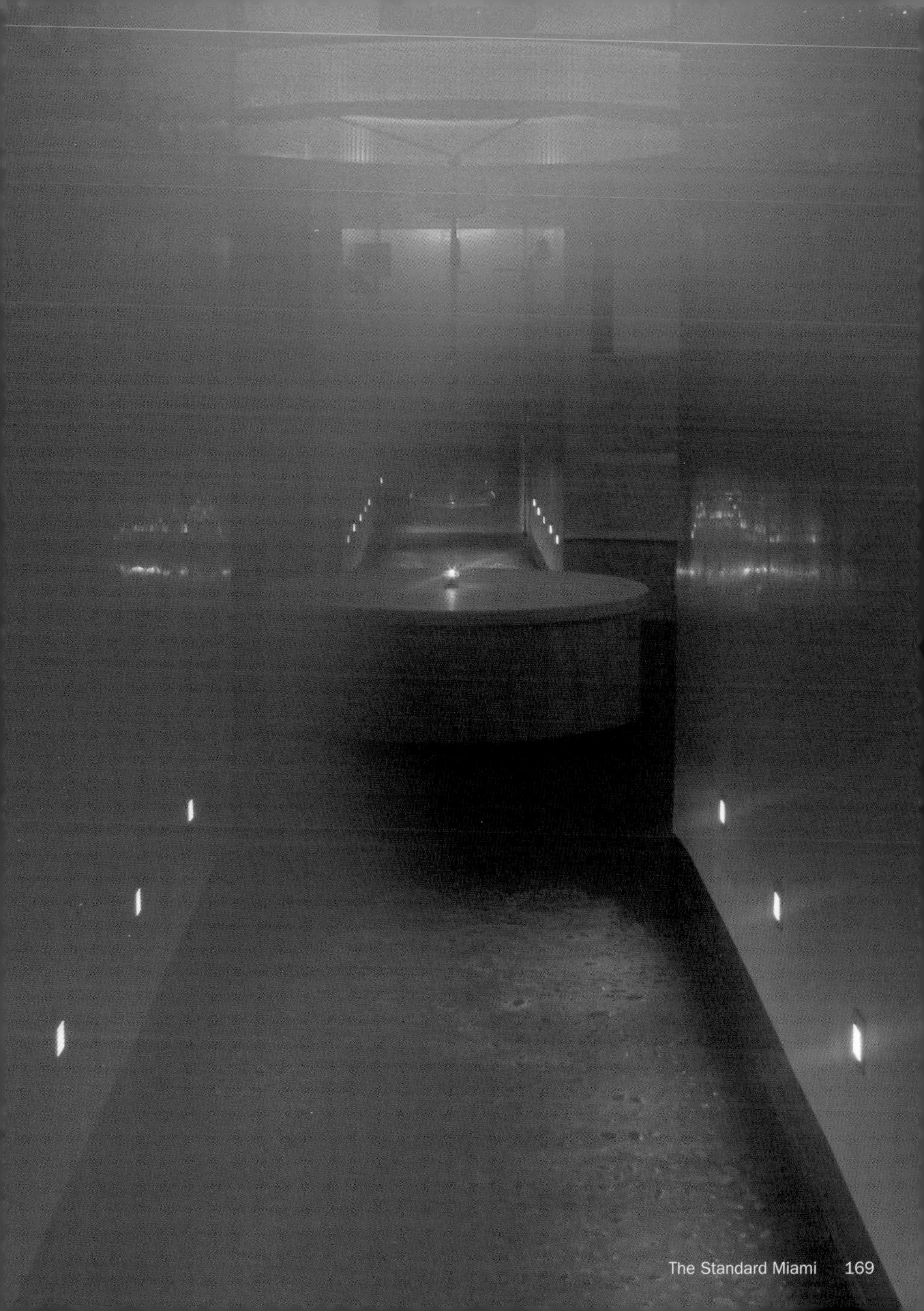

The Standard Miami

The Tides Riviera Maya

Playa Del Carmen
77710 Quintana Roo
Mexico
Phone: +529848773000
Fax: +523107520960
www.tidesrivieramaya.com

Price category: $$$$
Rooms: 30 villas
Facilities: "La Marea" restaurant, lounge, grill at the pool, lagoon pool with sundeck, "Maya Spa" with "Temzacal Sweat Lounge", boating, snorkeling, scuba diving, yoga
Services: Service team for guests of the "Royal Villas", the "Presidential Villa" and those with VIP status; maya jungle culinary experience with chef Ortiz, maya wedding ceremony, luxury car rentals
Located: 15 minutes north of Playa del Carmen and 50 minutes south of Cancun International Airport
Map: No. 30
Style: Tropical
What's special: Nestled in the tropical forest, this resort features exclusive private villas over 90 m² and an outdoor terrace replete with chaise lounge, dining area, handmade crochet hammock and outdoor shower.

Amanyara

Northwest Point, Providenciales
Turks and Caicos Islands
British West Indies
Phone: +16499418133
Fax: +16499418132
www.amanresorts.com

Price category: $$$$
Rooms: 40 pavilions and 33 residential villas
Facilities: Restaurant, bar, beach club, swimming pool, library, boutique, multimedia screening room, fitness center, tennis courts
Services: Internet access
Located: 25 minutes from Providenciales International Airport
Map: No. 31
Style: Modern classic
What's special: This secluded resort has 40 timber-shingle pavilions and 33 residential villas with sliding glass windows; activities include diving, tennis, and golf, as well as unique spa experiences such as body treatments and massages in the privacy of your own villa.

Carlisle Bay

Carlisle Bay, Old Road
Antigua
British West Indies
Phone: +12684840000
Fax: +12684840001
www.carlisle-bay.com

Price category: $$$$
Rooms: 82 suites
Facilities: 2 restaurants, 3 bars, "Blue Spa", sauna, plunge pool, 9 tennis courts, gymnasium, screening room, library, hair salon, cool kids club
Services: Daily afternoon tea, internet access
Located: 20 minutes from Antigua International Airport
Map: No. 32
Style: Contemporary design
What's special: This contemporary resort includes original art and photography, a private movie screening room, and a fully-stocked library. The 1,530 m² "Blue Spa" has six luxurious spa rooms for unique aromatherapy treatments.

Hotel Saint-Barth Isle de France

BP 612
97098 Saint-Barthélémy
French West Indies
Phone: +590590276181
Fax: +590590278683
www.isle-de-france.com

Price category: $$$$
Rooms: 33 rooms
Facilities: Restaurant, fresh water pools, spa, full gymnasium, tennis court, boutique
Services: Fashion shows every Tuesday
Located: 5 minutes from the airport
Map: No. 33
Style: Modern classic
What's special: Set on a pristine white sand beach this resort offers a wide variety of activities such as tennis, a fully equipped fitness center, and "Molton Brown Spa" with therapies individually tailored to your current state-of-mind.

Kempinski Hotel Colony Park Plaza

Rambla de las Americas & JM
Blanes
Colonia del Sacramento
Uruguay
Hotel: +5985226280
Info: +541148077008(110)
www.colonyparkplaza.com.ar

Price category: $$$$
Rooms: 68 rooms
Facilities: "Colony" restaurant, "Equilibrium Spa" with
outdoor and indoor pools, jet tub, sauna and gym, con-
ference and banqueting facilities for up to 300 people
Services: 24h room service, laundry, 24h concierge
service, multilingual staff, WiFi in public area, babysitting
on request
Located: 50-minutes drive to Buenos Aires International
Airport, 1.5-hours drive to Montevideo International Airport
Map: No. 34
Style: Modern country chic
What's special: This modern resort with its Feng Shui
design is set among 8,000 m² of lush gardens and is a
real oasis for the body and spirit; the 2,500 m² wellness
spa is devoted to state-of-the-art fitness training, beauty
treatments, and nutritional counseling.

Faena Hotel + Universe

Martha Salotti 445
Buenos Aires
Argentina
Phone: +541140109000
Fax: +541140109001
www.faenahotelanduniverse.com

Price category: $$$$
Rooms: 110 rooms
Facilities: "El Bistro" and "El Mercado" Restaurants with award-winning Spanish chef Mariano Cid de la Paz, cabaret with live performances, spa and hammam, outdoor pool and fully equipped gym
Services: Internet access, 24h personal Experience Managers
Located: 40 minutes to Ezeiza International Airport, 20 minutes to Jorge Newbery Airport
Map: No. 35
Style: Luxurious
What's special: Philippe Starck designed this ultra-hip hotel complete with a 21st century Baroque fun house. The luxury spa injects a healthy dose of spirituality with individualized sessions that revitalize the body's energetic aura.

Remota

Ruta 9 Norte, km 1.5
Puerto Natales
Chile
Phone: +5661414040
www.remota.cl

Price category: $$$$
Rooms: 72 rooms
Facilities: Restaurant (international and Chilean cuisine), bar, solarium, spot massages
Services: 24h room service, daily excursions: treks, hikes, horse back rides, and motor sailing in Patagonia National Park and Torres del Paine National Park
Located: International flights to Santiago, then flight to Punta Arenas
Map: No. 36
Style: Modern country chic
What's special: The secluded location and hotel's architecture is an invitation to stop and meditate; the spa includes a Finnish sauna, heated swimming pool, an open-air jacuzzi, and massages in a specially conditioned room.

Remota ▸ 219

No.	Hotel	Page
1	The Grove	10
2	Stoke Park Club	16
3	Gräflicher Park Hotel & Spa	20
4	Villa Kennedy	26
5	Side	32
6	Kempinski Grand Hotel	36
7	Bayerischer Hof	42
8	Grand Spa Resort A-ROSA Kitzbühel	46
9	Schwarzer Adler	50
10	wine & spa resort LOISIUM Hotel	58
11	Grand Hotel Bellevue	62
12	Victoria Jungfrau	66
13	Therme Vals	72
14	vigilius mountain resort	76
15	Adam & Eve Hotels	80
16	Amanjena	86
17	The Oberoi Udaivilas	92
18	Saman Villas	98

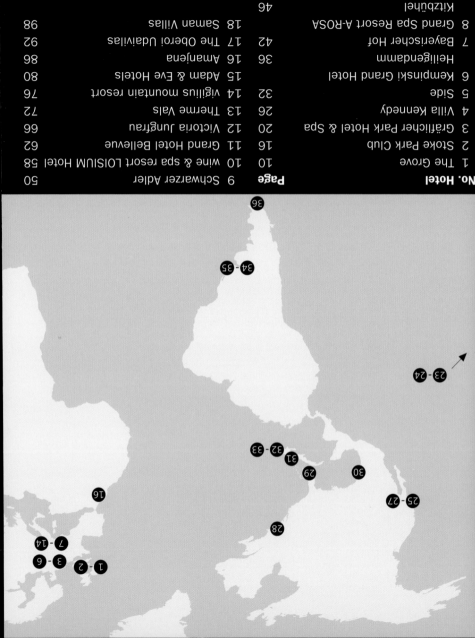

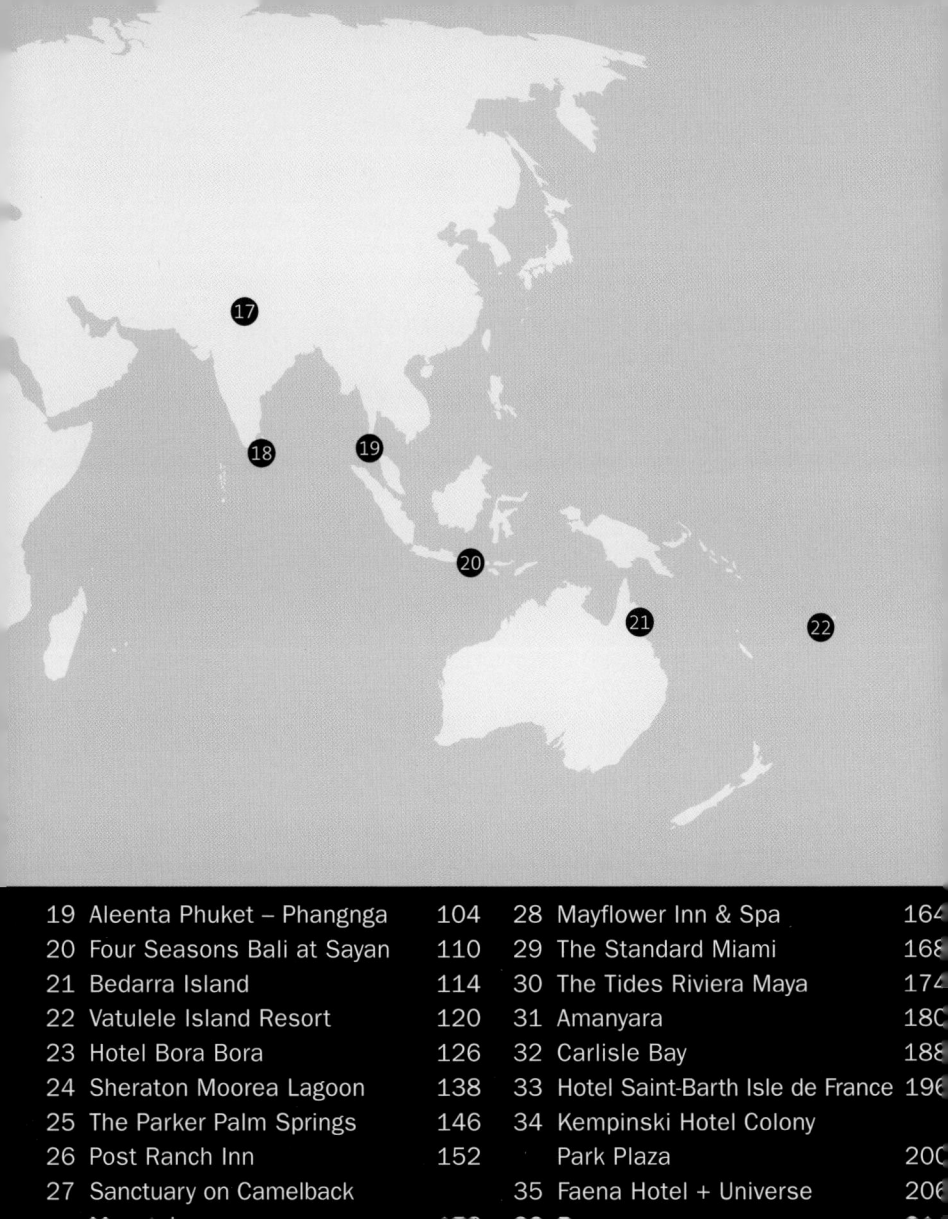

19 Aleenta Phuket – Phangnga   104

20 Four Seasons Bali at Sayan   110

21 Bedarra Island   114

22 Vatulele Island Resort   120

23 Hotel Bora Bora   126

24 Sheraton Moorea Lagoon   138

25 The Parker Palm Springs   146

26 Post Ranch Inn   152

27 Sanctuary on Camelback

28 Mayflower Inn & Spa   164

29 The Standard Miami   168

30 The Tides Riviera Maya   174

31 Amanyara   180

32 Carlisle Bay   188

33 Hotel Saint-Barth Isle de France   196

34 Kempinski Hotel Colony
Park Plaza   200

35 Faena Hotel + Universe   206

Other titles by teNeues

StyleGuides

Cool Hotels
London

ISBN 978-3-8327-9206-0

Cool Hotels
New York

ISBN 978-3-8327-9207-7

Cool Hotels
Paris

ISBN 978-3-8327-9205-3

Cool Hotels
Italy

ISBN 978-3-8327-9234-3

Cool Hotels
Spain

ISBN 978-3-8327-9230-5

Cool Hotels
Spa & Wellness

ISBN 978-3-8327-9243-5

Ecological Design

ISBN 978-3-8327-9229-9

Ecological Houses

ISBN 978-3-8327-9227-5

Garden Design

ISBN 978-3-8327-9228-2

Size: **15 x 19 cm**, 6 x 7½ in., 224 pp., **Flexicover**, c. 280 color photographs,
Text: English / German / French / Spanish / Italian

www.teneues.com

Other titles by teNeues

Cool Hotels

Cool Hotels
ISBN 978-3-8327-9105-6

Cool Hotels
Africa/Middle East
ISBN 978-3-8327-9051-6

Cool Hotels
America
ISBN 978-3-8238-4565-2

Cool Hotels
Cool Prices
ISBN 978-3-8327-9134-6

Cool Hotels
Ecological
ISBN 978-3-8327-9135-3

Cool Hotels
Family & Kids
ISBN 978-3-8327-9203-9

Size: **13.5 x 19 cm**, 5¼ x 7½ in., **Flexicover**, c. 400 pp., 400 color photographs,
Text: English / German / French / Spanish / Italian

Cool Restaurants

Cool Restaurants
Berlin
ISBN 978-3-8238-4585-0

Cool Restaurants
Cape Town
ISBN 978-3-8327-9103-2

Cool Restaurants
Copenhagen
ISBN 978-3-8327-9146-9

Size: **14.6 x 22.5 cm**, 5¾ x 8¾ in., **Flexicover**, c. 136 pp., 130 color photographs,
Text: English / German / French / Spanish / Italian

www.teneues.com

Other titles by teNeues

Cool Restaurants

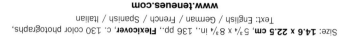

Cool Restaurants
Moscow

ISBN 978-3-8327-9147-6

Cool Restaurants
Miami

ISBN 978-3-8327-9066-0

Cool Restaurants
Frankfurt

ISBN 978-3-8327-9118-6

Cool Restaurants
San Francisco

ISBN 978-3-8327-9067-7

Cool Restaurants
Prague

ISBN 978-3-8327-9068-4

Cool Restaurants
New York

ISBN 978-3-8327-9232-9

Cool Spots

COOL SPOTS
SALZBURG/
KITZBÜHEL

ISBN 978-3-8327-9177-3

COOL SPOTS
LAS VEGAS

ISBN 978-3-8327-9152-0

COOL SPOTS
CÔTE D'AZUR

ISBN 978-3-8327-9154-4

Size: **14.6 x 22.5 cm**, 5 ¾ x 8 ⅞ in., 136 pp., **Flexicover**, c. 130 color photographs,
Text: English / German / French / Spanish / Italian

www.teneues.com